One

Lauren Strang

for the one that was worth the wait

you have my heart

the ONE who came first

I still dream of you sometimes

replaying those days

when we were young and in love

and thought everything mattered

much more than it really did

I wish I had relished

the feel of your hand in mine

more than the hurtful words that were said

as it crumbled

I never thought about it much

at the time

me and her

my first real love

that she was a she

and I was a her

like it didn't need second guessing

she was a person

I was a person

we were in love

but when people ask

who was your first?

it isn't her name I speak

it is the one that came after

the boy

when they ask me my number

I say

five

no

six

well it depends

does it count?

did she count?

did I look into those brown eyes

and feel the softness of her flesh

beneath my fingertips

thinking she didn't count

no

we were imperfect

we were young

they said to me

at the time

she is just a phase

but I can't help but think

a love like that

young though it was

naive though it was

could never have been a phase

nothing prepares you

for when

that first flush of golden warmth

turns to ice

first love

is sitting back

years later

and realising

it was never really

love at all

the sun kissed days

of I heart ?

on the back of hands

in the margins of school notes

trying to keep the secret

but hoping they will ask

those summer weekends

spent wishing they will be around

just so you can spend an hour or two

dancing around each other

unsure of what the feeling

in the pit of your stomach is

dizzy whispers to friends

who make transparent remarks

as they pass by

so your face flushes bright red

and you know the embarrassment

will follow you always

heartbroken tears in bathroom stalls

surrounded by girls

promising you

he is not worth it

as if any of you

really know what love is anyway

-       simpler times

the ONE that hurt

there is a difference

between the girl I was at eighteen

when I thought I needed you

and the girl I was at twenty-two

when I knew I didn't

and you hated it

I often ask myself

if I have made too much

of the ways he hurt me

that it wasn't as bad as I make out

maybe he did love me

isn't that what relationships are like after all?

but

then I remember

the night I sobbed into my pillow

and he rolled over and told me

he was too tired to deal with me

the time he let his family make me cry

and didn't say a word in my defence

the way he told me

over and over

until it was so seared in my brain

that I even believe it now

that no one could ever love me except him

that no one has the patience

that I talk to much

20

I laugh too loud

I overexaggerate my feelings

that when I am upset with him

it is because I'm not good enough

there are the half remembered the nights

I would wake to him above me

fear caught in my throat

there are the ways he would pretend in public

but remind me of the truth when we were alone

but

he never hit me

he never injured me

so it can't have been all bad

right?

you only loved me

when I needed you

as soon as I found

any sense of freedom

confidence

you squashed it

so I would lean on you again

and could not leave

what I thought was love

turned out to be control

he left scars but none of them are visible

he didn't like it

when I sang

and so

I was silenced

your love poisoned me

from the inside out

searing through my blood like acid

bubbling to the surface

until I was nothing but

a burnt-out shell

a woman I did not recognise

believing that no one could want me

because I was broken

and trusting that love was supposed to sting

I would smile and tell them

how much I loved you

how good we were

I would roll my eyes and laugh

at the annoying things you would do

I would tell myself

over

and over

how I couldn't be without you

but at night

when you lay next to me, back turned

I would cry myself to sleep silently

wondering how I had gotten myself

trapped in a life I did not want

with a man I no longer loved

it was the right thing to do

but I still cried when I left

it is when you look at your life

and feel nothing

that you know

the love is gone

it has taken me a long time to realise

that so much of who I am today

are defences I created

so that you could hurt me

and I would stay

the venom in his voice

when he said

you don't love me anymore, do you?

shrank me back into myself

and I almost retreated

I almost lied

afraid

not for the first time

of the hate in his eyes

but I still said

no

even if it only came out as a whisper

-finding my courage in fear

how many times will I make you apologise

before the words sound less

like a plea

and more like a promise?

you say you love me

in such unobtrusive ways

so subtle

they bleed through my fingers

like water

yet

I don't think you have it in you

to love

you won't allow even a crack

in the hard prison

you have built around your heart

but

I think I got closer

than you would like to admit

how quickly

arms that were once a safe place to land

can become a dangerous place to lay your heart

with just a few words

here you linger

on the edges of the echoes

of my dreams

a ghost without a shadow

that I have not yet learned to evade

a reminder

of the claws you dug into my skin

rendering me raw and wounded

long after you slunk back

into the shades of my nightmares

I give and I give

until I am a hollowed husk

and you

sit gorged and ripe

your cup brimming with my love

tell me how

I am supposed to sit across from you

and pretend

that I don't love every moment of you

do you keep count

of the hearts you broke before mine?

I wonder when you will realise

that all these tears

-shed and unshed

held until I couldn't breathe-

are for you

I wonder if you would even care

how is it

that you make me feel

like I am too much

and not enough

all at once

the years since I left tick by

and I wonder

how am I so damaged?

what did I do wrong to feel this pain?

until one day

the pieces slot together

and I realise the wounds that haven't healed

were opened and poisoned

by you

because of you

for you

and I am left festering

even in your absence

my heart beats

feeble and slow

ripped down the centre

a vicious gash

put there by him

by time

by my own self-loathing

you take my heart

so softly in your palm

handing me a needle and thread

guiding my hand

so I lean on you

and I stich the wound back together

slow

messy

until it beats strong

and I can barely notice the cotton in the flesh

once I am done

and whole again

you hand my heart back

take your scissors

and unpick each thread

until my heart is once again splayed

and raw

ravaged by fresh wounds

left by my own foolish trust

have you not taken enough of my sleepless nights?
must you haunt my waking steps too?

you are making a mountain out of a molehill

was his favourite thing to say to me

so now

every mountain

is a molehill

and even when I am drowning

I will swear blind I can touch the bottom

I refuse you

any more space

on my blank pages

the ONE that wasn't meant to be

fuck

-       the first word I said when I realised I
        loved you

with my rain

and your thunder

the storms are inevitable

and they fill the sky

with lightening

how many hours must I waste

staring at the ceiling

trying not to think about you

how many sleepless nights must I spend

restless and hoping

that you are trying not to think about me

I was strong before you

I will be strong after you

but somehow

I must navigate

the in-between

in which

you have me hostage

I think that what is broken in me

fits around what is broken in you

and together we are a patchwork

sewn in haste

trying desperately to hold each other whole

even as the edges fray

his eyes flicker to my lips

for a fraction

of a heartbeat

and I can feel the electric current

vibrate in the air beneath

all of our what ifs

and I think

we might always be

a little bit

in love

I love you

why isn't that enough?

one day being in love with you

will hurt less

but I dread that moment

the pain of loving you

the only thing reminding me

that once

you loved me too

I am lost

in a labyrinth

of what ifs

and maybes

isn't it disquieting

to realise

that you were the other girl

all along

to be heartbroken over you

is to feel a gut punch

whenever you smile

but wanting you to smile all the same

it is a razor-sharp pain in my chest

when I hear your laugh

but replaying the sound over and over

it is swollen held back tears

as your wrap your arms around me

but craving your touch still

and never wanting you to let go

we convinced no one

our love radiated from us

and bathed them in gold

the nudges and the side glances

left us unfazed

the whispers that followed us

fell on ears already full of the bliss

of murmured sweet nothings

fools in love

that should have seen the world

for its truth

and not under the guise

of happy ever after

the hardest part is knowing

she is the one you will see your face

in flickering candlelight

at 2am

as you lay entwined and content

no amount of dreaming

will bring you back to me

no amount of dreaming

will unbreak my heart

no amount of dreaming

can make you love me

the way I have always loved you

maybe our time will come

when we are different

when our lives are not so complicated

maybe one day we will find our way back

into each other's arms

I think

even then

we will still love each other

maybe, when the time is right

I will hold you again

and wonder

why we waited so long

I have been in love before

felt the sting of rejection

the way the heart can crack in a single moment

the way you feel like you can never

put yourself back together

but nothing prepared me

for my heart

to feel so swollen with love

whilst shattered like stain glass

so that all I am left with

the constant need to be held by you

and the constant desire to never see you again

my shattered, swollen heart

can't seem to decide

which one

will cause me more pain

halfway across the world

and he doesn't know

that when they ask

what my biggest regret is

it is his name

that tumbles from my lips

I was afraid you would never love me
you were terrified that you already did

we knew the risks

but we fell in love anyway

and when it became too much

you changed your mind

pretended to take back the way you looked at me

when we woke in each other's arms

the feel of your hand tipping my chin

as you lean in for a kiss

unspoken words lingering in the air between us

but I know

I know even now

the cost was high

but the love was worth it

and I would do it again

without the question even needing to be asked

stealing secret kisses

in secret corridors

hiding secret heartbreak

under secret smiles

in my dreams

had you asked

I would have given it all up

just to wake curled beside you

I knew

it would not last

that our time was finite

and yet

I let myself fall

as if the desperation of wanting you

was enough to catch me

but all I ended with were bruises

and a love so intense

that I am still tumbling

as you watch from above

your hand clutched around my bleeding heart

I am in love

with the fantasy of a future

I built around you

forgetting the reality

of her

I am a drama queen

and you are a stubborn arse

it never could have worked

but fuck, I loved you anyway

no one knows

but us

no one notices

the way you look at me across the room

asking silently if you

will kiss me again

no one feels the tension

that crackles the air

when we are mere inches apart

no one notices the way you brush your hand

across my waist

in the darkness of the bar

no one can tell

that I think about taking you home

as I dance in his arms

it's funny how the words

'I made a mistake'

always come too late

all this love

swelling inside me

until I am bloated

searching desperately

for a place to release it

it is intense

that falling feeling

when you look into his eyes

and the world opens beneath your feet

and as you drop

spinning further away from the light

it occurs to you

That you won't be the same person

when you hit the ground

the girl you knew is gone

replaced

by one who is parched for the taste of him

who runs her fingers over her skin

imagining it is his touch that sets her alight

you have looked in the mirror

and see the change he has wrought

in the very depths of you

he took a girl made of sunshine

and turned her to fire

it hurts

to love you

it always has

if I could snap my fingers

take us back to the moment before it went wrong

I would

in less time than it takes

for my chest to rise and fall

breathing you in

but

I can't fix the mess you made

and now

I must learn to love you less

or love you differently

or lose you completely

so I spend restless nights

trying to extinguish the pain of missing you

and maybe I will be telling you

that I love you

forever

and maybe it will never hurt any less

but maybe

one day

I will learn

how to love you the right way

and be around you without feeling empty

missing you

is like drowning

in air

the romantic in me

hopes you look up at the stars

and wonder

if I look at them too

I think of all those movies

we never saw in their entirety

end credits playing as we are a tangle of limbs

and wonder

if I'll ever watch them in the same way again

the bittersweet scent

of our love affair

lingers in the shadows

like smoke

the ONE that was worth the wait

he arrived in my life

like a tornado

crashing through and ripping up

everything I had built

and worked so hard to convince myself

was good

until I realised

the foundations had been cracked all along

and it was only a matter of time

before it crumbled beneath my feet

when I uncurled myself

and picked my way out of the rubble

I was no longer afraid of

what he had made me feel

so when he reached out his hand

and asked me to run away with him

I left the wreckage behind

I don't believe in love at first sight

I don't believe in soulmates

but I do believe

that from the first moment I met you

I knew you would be something extraordinary

I never knew what it felt like

to truly be seen

until you looked at me

that first soft touch

sent electricity through my veins

awakening parts of me I hadn't known existed

and left me

thrumming for days

on those days

when I feel empty

and misunderstood

wishing for sleep for no other reason

than a moment of quiet

you wrap your arms around me

and remind me of my own power

that I am strong

brave

worthy

and capable of taking your hand

to pull myself out of my nightmares

we joke that you saved me

but

it is not true

you showed me

that I could save myself

that I am

worthy

and brave

and capable

and already everything

you could ever love

sometimes I look at you

and wonder when I will awake from the dream

but when I open my eyes

you look back at me a smile

and I know that my dream

is our reality

.

when you laugh

my whole world brightens

and I ache to be part of your joy

even for a moment

because a moment of your joy

is enough

to warm me for life

in the moments we are apart

I think of being

stretched out on the sofa

lazily trailing kisses along your jaw

running my fingers through your hair

putting my head to your chest

and breathing in time to your heartbeat

close and safe and warm

and never wanting it to end

when I realised I could be myself

my true self

and you would love me still

not in spite of it

but because of it

I knew I had found

the one

even if we parted ways

I would remember the laughter

there are millions of people in this world
and many of them I could love
but I would choose you every time
regardless

somewhere between

the feel of your fingers tracing my spine

the way you looked at me

with just a glimmer of surprise

and the goofy smile that lights up your face

I fell in love

remind me again

of all the ways you love me

I am afraid

I might forget

no matter if

the world burns around us

I know

I can always come home to you

and we will warm ourselves over the flames

hand in hand

bookshops

thunderstorms

the smell of fresh baked bread

sunsets over the sea

you

-     things that make me happy

video games

coffee

cute animals

dancing in fields at festivals

me

\-   things that make you happy

it is late night snacks and blanket forts

it is surprise sunflowers and tomato plants

it is reaching for a hand under the covers whilst
you sleep

it is tattered leggings and that one awful shirt

it is asking what is for dinner every day

it is lazy Sundays in bed and reluctant Monday
mornings

it is hysterics on train journeys and tears at
sad movies

it is stupid voices and kisses at the supermarket
checkout

it is listening to rants and laughing at mistakes

it is craving attention and asking to be left
alone

it is ordering takeout and watching that movie
you said you never would

it is choosing baked beans over a restaurant

it is talking about fears and dreaming about
hopes

it is waiting to watch the next episode

it is making hot chocolate at midnight

it is sending silly pictures and shopping lists

it is being wrapped up warm on a cold night

it is a safe place to settle when the world feels too much

it is real

it is love

it is you

he reignited feelings

that had turned to ash

and so I burned everything down

for a flicker

of his warmth

once the fire

was nothing but embers

and my life razed to the ground

he stood there in the smoke

ready to help me rebuild

the ONE

the terror in your eyes

when you said

I can't lose anyone else

was enough

to show me

that I am worthy of life

I am worthy of love

you can take responsibility

for the mistakes you made

without blaming yourself

for the way he hurt you

at least if my heart is cracked

it can never be accused

of not being open

I spent life searching

thinking that someone else

would be the key to my happiness

only to realise

it was already unlocked

within me

I am not a half

waiting for another

to complete me

I don't have to bathe in self-love
to be worthy of love from others
but I do have to realise
that I am already worthy
of love from myself

we spend our whole lives

being told

that romantic love is the thing to aspire to

yet

the purest love

comes from within

and that settles the soul

far greater than any other person could

there is a girl

she stands on the edge of a cliff

waves crashing below her

thinking

is this my life

she winds through the years

in her mind

the ones she gave to me

who could not love her

and opinions that did not matter

time spend trying to fit

into smaller clothes

and change who she was

just for a kernel of affection

because that was what she was taught

that is how she assumed life worked

so many missed moments

because she was wrapped up

in the judgement of others

she could not see the light

that spilled out from her

one bad word

was enough to erase fifty good

and any moment of weakness

threw her strengths into darkness

and when she was deepest

in that shadow world

no amount of declarations of love

or words of comfort and encouragement

could reach her

now, as the cold sea spray

dapples her skin

and her toes flex on the edge of the sheer drop

she understands

none of that matters

she can chase away those dark monsters

that haunt her footsteps

with the power of her own voice

the conviction of her own heart

and the love of her own soul

keep your heart soft

the bruises may run deeper

it may cause you pain

but my god

there will be so much love

don't dim your shine

for a boy covered in dust

if love leaves you unhappy

then it isn't really love at all

and you deserve love

even if it looks a little different than expected

especially if it comes from within

sweet girl

one day you will realise

that you were always enough

and never too much

and the only people who would tell you otherwise

are not worth

a fraction

of your precious life

Printed in Great Britain
by Amazon